Usborne
Times
Tables
Practice Pad

Written by Sam Smith

Designed by Karen Tomlins
and Gregor Laird

Once you've completed an activity sheet from this pad, you
can check your answers using the list of tables at the back.
There's also a multiplication grid and some useful tips at
the back to help you remember each times table.

Count the dots

Use the sets of dots next to each calculation to help you count to each number in the 2x table. Write the answers in the circles.

1 x 2 = (2)

2 x 2 = ( )

3 x 2 = ( )

4 x 2 = ( )

5 x 2 = ( )

6 x 2 = ( )

7 x 2 = ( )

8 x 2 = ( )

9 x 2 = ( )

10 x 2 = ( )

11 x 2 = ( )

12 x 2 = ( )

Dove pairs

Count up the doves in twos. Follow the arrows,
and write the new total under each pair.

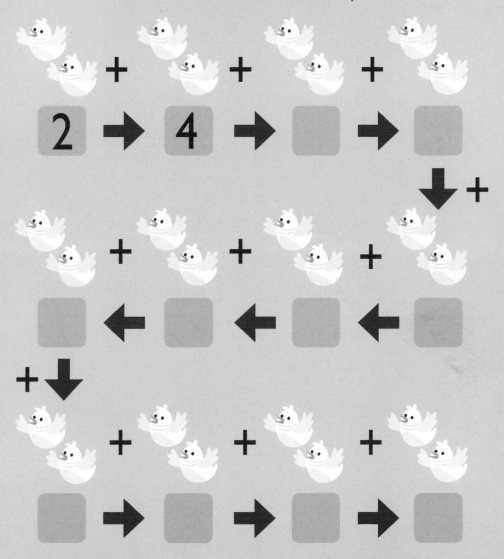

Missing numbers

2x

Fill in the missing numbers to complete the 2x table.

$1 \times 2 = 2$

$7 \times 2 = \bigcirc$

$2 \times \bigcirc = 4$

$\bigcirc \times 2 = 16$

$\bigcirc \times 2 = 6$

$9 \times \bigcirc = 18$

$4 \times 2 = \bigcirc$

$10 \times 2 = \bigcirc$

$\bigcirc \times 2 = 10$

$11 \times 2 = \bigcirc$

$6 \times 2 = \bigcirc$

$\bigcirc \times 2 = 24$

Sock pairs

Write the number of pairs of socks in each group.
Then write the total number of socks in each group.

 2 pairs

4 socks

 pairs

socks

 pairs

socks

 pairs

socks

Empty boxes

Write the missing numbers in the boxes to complete these multiplications.

$2 \times \boxed{} = 10$

$8 \times 2 = \boxed{}$

$\boxed{} \times 2 = 24$

$2 \times \boxed{} = 4$

$\boxed{} \times 2 = 20$

$2 \times 7 = \boxed{}$

Number wheel

Fill in the blank sections of the number wheel so that multiplying the number in the inner ring by two gives the number in the outer ring.

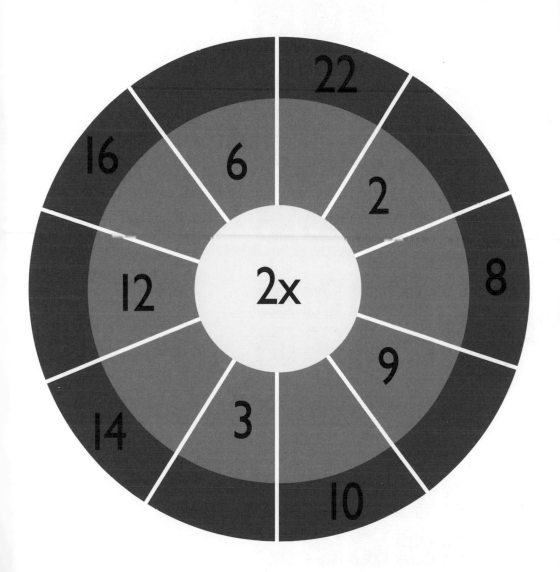

Dice dots

Change these groups of twos into 2x table multiplication facts.

Example: = 3 x 2 = 6

 = ... X .... = ...

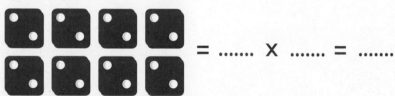 = ... X .... = ...

= .... X .... = ...

 = ... X .... = ...

 = ... X .... = ...

Multiplying machines

Fill in the boxes to complete all of the multiplications by two.

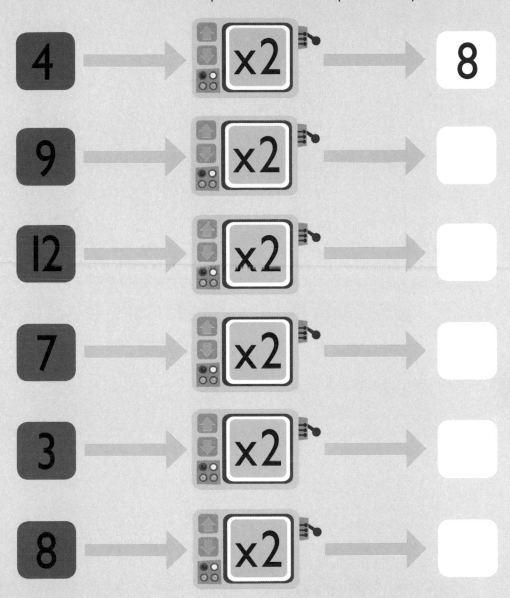

4 → x2 → 8

9 → x2 →

12 → x2 →

7 → x2 →

3 → x2 →

8 → x2 →

Word problems

Use the 2x table to solve these word problems,
and write your answers in the boxes.

There are twelve months in a year.
How many months are there in two years?

A T-shirt has two sleeves.
How many sleeves do seven T-shirts have?

Paul is twice as old as his nephew, who is eight.
How old is Paul?

There are two wheels on a bicycle.
How many wheels are there on five bicycles?

To make a cake you need two eggs.
How many eggs do you need to make nine cakes?

Empty boxes

Write the missing numbers in the boxes to complete these multiplications.

$6 \times 2 = \boxed{}$

$2 \times \boxed{} = 18$

$\boxed{} \times 2 = 22$

$2 \times \boxed{} = 8$

$\boxed{} \times 2 = 14$

$3 \times 2 = \boxed{}$

Speed calculations

Write down the answers to these calculations as quickly as you can.
See if you can finish them all in two minutes.

3 x 2 = ◯   2 x 10 = ◯

2 x 12 = ◯   2 x 2 = ◯

5 x 2 = ◯   8 x 2 = ◯

7 x 2 = ◯   2 x 3 = ◯

2 x 9 = ◯   11 x 2 = ◯

6 x 2 = ◯   2 x 5 = ◯

1 x 2 = ◯   12 x 2 = ◯

2 x 11 = ◯   2 x 7 = ◯

4 x 2 = ◯   9 x 2 = ◯

Count the dots

Use the sets of dots next to each calculation to help you count to
each number in the 3x table. Write the answers in the circles.

$1 \times 3 =$ (3)

$2 \times 3 =$ ( )

$3 \times 3 =$ ( )

$4 \times 3 =$ ( )

$5 \times 3 =$ ( )

$6 \times 3 =$ ( )

$7 \times 3 =$ ( )

$8 \times 3 =$ ( )

$9 \times 3 =$ ( )

$10 \times 3 =$ ( )

$11 \times 3 =$ ( )

$12 \times 3 =$ ( )

Mice threes

Count up the mice in threes. Follow the arrows,
and write the new total under each group.

Missing numbers

Fill in the missing numbers to complete the 3x table.

$1 \times 3 = 3$ $\bigcirc \times 3 = 21$

$\bigcirc \times 3 = 6$ $8 \times 3 = \bigcirc$

$3 \times 3 = \bigcirc$ $9 \times \bigcirc = 27$

$4 \times \bigcirc = 12$ $10 \times 3 = \bigcirc$

$5 \times 3 = \bigcirc$ $\bigcirc \times 3 = 33$

$\bigcirc \times 3 = 18$ $12 \times 3 = \bigcirc$

Traffic signals

Write the number of sets of lights in each group.
Then write the total number of lights in each group.

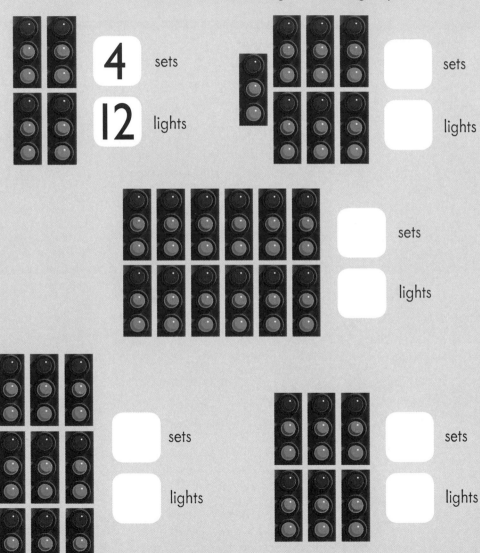

4 sets

12 lights

sets

lights

sets

lights

sets

lights

sets

lights

Empty boxes

Write the missing numbers in the boxes to complete these multiplications.

$\boxed{} \times 3 = 12$

$3 \times 7 = \boxed{}$

$3 \times \boxed{} = 9$

$\boxed{} \times 3 = 33$

$5 \times 3 = \boxed{}$

$3 \times \boxed{} = 27$

Number wheel

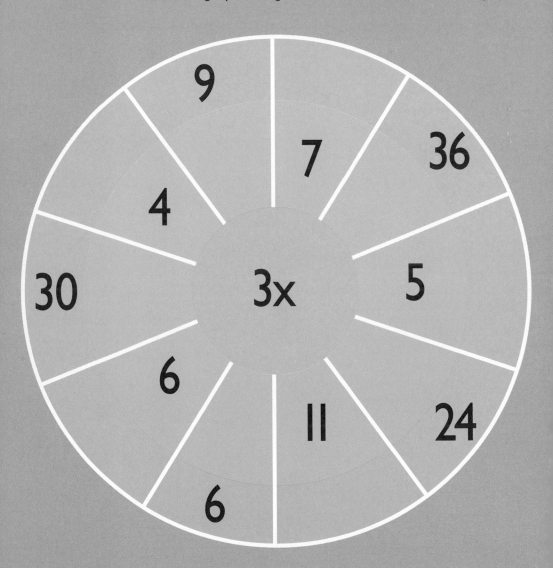

3x

Fill in the blank sections of the number wheel so that multiplying the number in the inner ring by three gives the number in the outer ring.

Dice dots

Change these groups of threes into 3x table multiplication facts.

Example: = 4 x 3 = 12

= .... X .... = ...

= .... X .... = ...

= .... X .... = ...

= .... X .... = ...

= .... X .... = ...

Multiplying machines

Fill in the boxes to complete all of the multiplications by three.

3 ⟶ x3 ⟶ 9

6 ⟶ x3 ⟶ ☐

10 ⟶ x3 ⟶ ☐

5 ⟶ x3 ⟶ ☐

8 ⟶ x3 ⟶ ☐

12 ⟶ x3 ⟶ ☐

Word problems

Use the 3x table to solve these word problems,
and write your answers in the boxes.

A triangle has three sides.
How many sides are there on six triangles?

There are eleven players in a sports team.
How many players are there in three sports teams?

There are three scoops of ice cream in a cone.
How many scoops would there be in five cones?

A bag contains eight oranges.
How many oranges are there in three bags?

A propeller has three blades.
How many blades are there on four propellers?

Empty boxes

Write the missing numbers in the boxes to complete these multiplications.

$3 \times 6 = \boxed{}$

$\boxed{} \times 3 = 30$

$2 \times 3 = \boxed{}$

$3 \times \boxed{} = 24$

$\boxed{} \times 3 = 36$

$3 \times \boxed{} = 15$

Speed calculations

Write down the answers to these calculations as quickly as you can.
See if you can finish them all in two minutes.

10 x 3 = ◯   3 x 3 = ◯

3 x 2 = ◯   11 x 3 = ◯

3 x 6 = ◯   3 x 4 = ◯

5 x 3 = ◯   3 x 9 = ◯

3 x 12 = ◯   7 x 3 = ◯

4 x 3 = ◯   3 x 8 = ◯

3 x 11 = ◯   3 x 1 = ◯

9 x 3 = ◯   12 x 3 = ◯

3 x 7 = ◯   3 x 5 = ◯

Count the dots

Use the sets of dots next to each calculation to help you count to each number in the 4x table. Write the answers in the circles.

1 x 4 = 4

2 x 4 = ◯

3 x 4 = ◯

4 x 4 = ◯

5 x 4 = ◯

6 x 4 = ◯

7 x 4 = ◯

8 x 4 = ◯

9 x 4 = ◯

10 x 4 = ◯

11 x 4 = ◯

12 x 4 = ◯

Snail fours

Count up the snails in fours. Follow the arrows,
and write the new total under each group.

| 4 | → | 8 | → | | → | |

| | ← | | ← | | ← | |

| | → | | → | | → | |

Missing numbers

4x

Fill in the missing numbers to complete the 4x table.

$1 \times 4 = 4$

$ \times 4 = 28$

$ \times 4 = 8$

$8 \times = 32$

$3 \times 4 = $

$9 \times 4 = $

$ \times 4 = 16$

$10 \times 4 = $

$5 \times = 20$

$ \times 4 = 44$

$6 \times 4 = $

$12 \times 4 = $

Windmill sails

Write the number of windmills in each group.
Then write the total number of sails in each group.

2 windmills

8 sails

windmills

sails

windmills

sails

windmills

sails

windmills

sails

Empty boxes

Write the missing numbers in the boxes to complete these multiplications.

4 x 10 = ☐

☐ x 4 = 8

12 x 4 = ☐

4 x ☐ = 12

☐ x 4 = 24

4 x ☐ = 32

Number wheel

Fill in the blank sections of the number wheel so that multiplying the number in the inner ring by four gives the number in the outer ring.

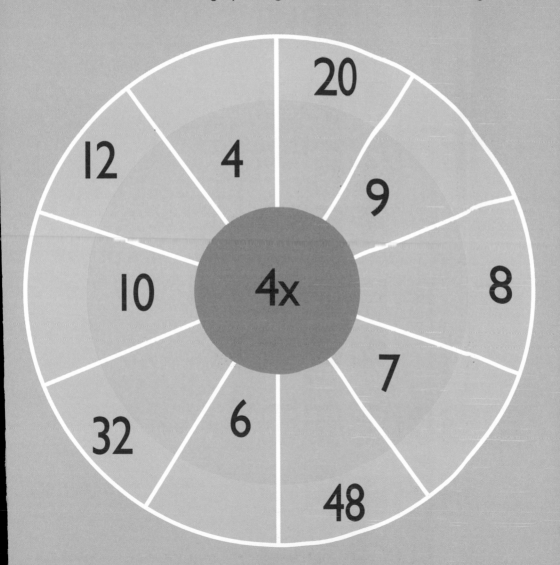

Dice dots

Change these groups of fours into 4x table multiplication facts.

Example: = 2 x 4 = 8

= .... X .... = ...

= .... X .... = ...

= .... X .... = ...

= .... X .... = ...

= .... X .... = ...

Multiplying machines

4x

Fill in the boxes to complete all of the multiplications by four.

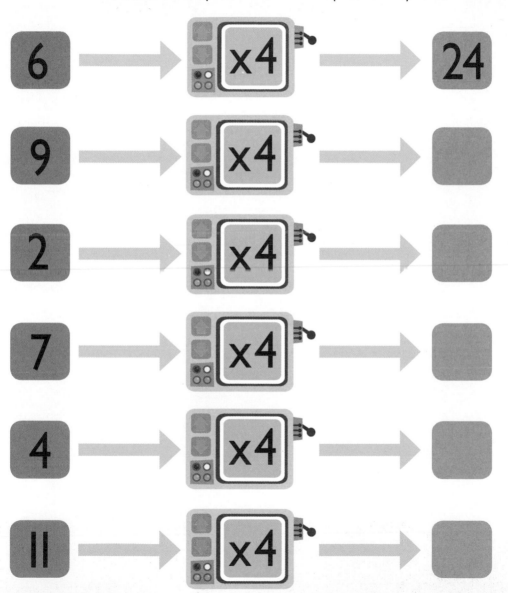

6 → x4 → 24

9 → x4 →

2 → x4 →

7 → x4 →

4 → x4 →

11 → x4 →

Word problems

Use the 4x table to solve these word problems,
and write your answers in the boxes.

Four friends each bring five tennis balls to a match.
How many tennis balls is that in total?

There are four wheels on a car.
How many wheels are there on nine cars?

A pack of pencils contains twelve pencils.
How many pencils are there in four packs?

There are four runners in a relay team.
How many runners are there in seven relay teams?

A house has four windows.
How many windows do eight houses have?

Empty boxes

Write the missing numbers in the boxes to complete these multiplications.

4 x ☐ = 20

☐ x 4 = 28

6 x 4 = ☐

☐ x 4 = 44

4 x 9 = ☐

4 x ☐ = 16

Speed calculations

Write down the answers to these calculations as quickly as you can.
See if you can finish them all in two minutes.

$7 \times 4 =$

$4 \times 12 =$

$6 \times 4 =$

$3 \times 4 =$

$4 \times 9 =$

$8 \times 4 =$

$10 \times 4 =$

$4 \times 2 =$

$4 \times 4 =$

$4 \times 11 =$

$9 \times 4 =$

$4 \times 8 =$

$1 \times 4 =$

$4 \times 5 =$

$12 \times 4 =$

$4 \times 3 =$

$4 \times 7 =$

$4 \times 6 =$

Count the dots

Use the sets of dots next to each calculation to help you count to each number in the 5x table. Write the answers in the circles.

1 x 5 = ⑤

2 x 5 = ◯

3 x 5 = ◯

4 x 5 = ◯

5 x 5 = ◯

6 x 5 = ◯

7 x 5 = ◯

8 x 5 = ◯

9 x 5 = ◯

10 x 5 = ◯

11 x 5 = ◯

12 x 5 = ◯

Counting cupcakes

Count up the cupcakes in fives. Follow the arrows,
and write the new total under each group.

5 → **10** → ☐ → ☐

☐ ← ☐ ← ☐ ←

☐ → ☐ → ☐ → ☐

Missing numbers

Fill in the missing numbers to complete the 5x table.

1 x 5 = (5)   7 x 5 = ( )

( ) x 5 = 10   ( ) x 5 = 40

3 x ( ) = 15   9 x 5 = ( )

4 x 5 = ( )   10 x ( ) = 50

5 x 5 = ( )   11 x 5 = ( )

( ) x 5 = 30   ( ) x 5 = 60

Starfish sets

Write the number of starfish in each group.
Then write the total number of arms in each group.

3 starfish

15 arms

starfish

arms

starfish

arms

starfish

arms

starfish

arms

Empty boxes

Write the missing numbers in the boxes to complete these multiplications.

□ x 5 = 45

5 x 2 = □

5 x □ = 25

□ x 5 = 60

5 x □ = 5

10 x 5 = □

Number wheel

Fill in the blank sections of the number wheel so that multiplying the number in the inner ring by five gives the number in the outer ring.

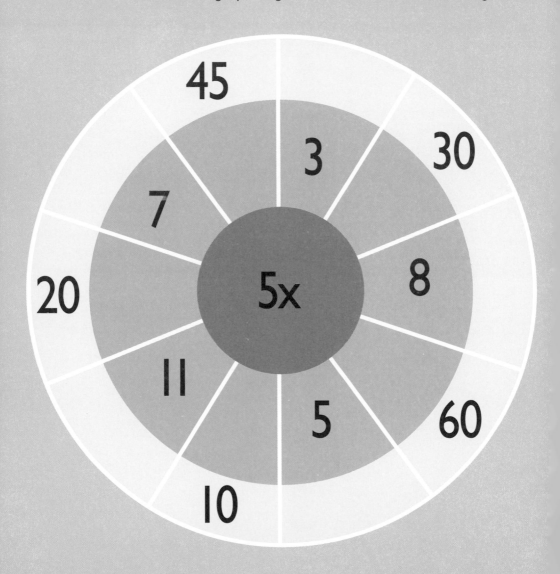

Dice dots

Change these groups of fives into 5x table multiplication facts.

Example: $\boxed{:\cdot:}$ $\boxed{:\cdot:}$ $\boxed{:\cdot:}$ = 3 x 5 = 15

= .... X .... = ...

= .... X .... = ...

= .... X .... = ...

= .... X .... = ...

= .... X .... = ...

Multiplying machines

Fill in the boxes to complete all of the multiplications by five.

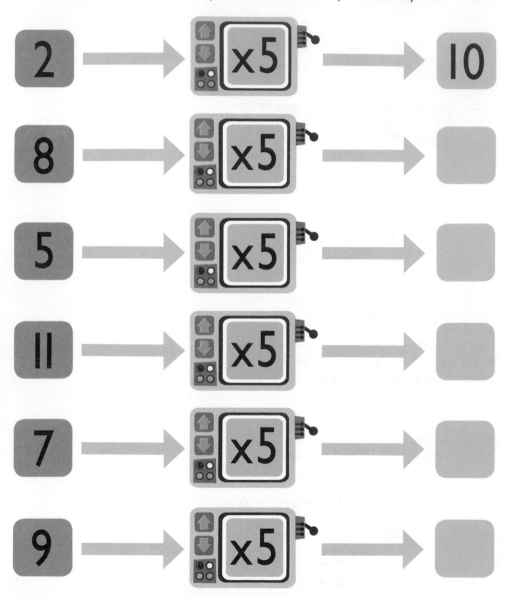

$2 \rightarrow \times 5 \rightarrow 10$

$8 \rightarrow \times 5 \rightarrow \square$

$5 \rightarrow \times 5 \rightarrow \square$

$11 \rightarrow \times 5 \rightarrow \square$

$7 \rightarrow \times 5 \rightarrow \square$

$9 \rightarrow \times 5 \rightarrow \square$

Word problems

Use the 5x table to solve these word problems,
and write your answers in the boxes.

There are five sides on a pentagon.
How many sides are there on eleven pentagons?

John works five days a week.
How many days does he work in seven weeks?

Five people can sit around a table.
How many people can sit around three tables?

A bag contains five cookies.
How many cookies are there in twelve bags?

It takes Laura five minutes to make a paper plane.
How long would it take her to make nine of them?

Empty boxes

Write the missing numbers in the boxes to complete these multiplications.

7 x 5 = ☐

5 x ☐ = 55

☐ x 5 = 40

5 x ☐ = 15

☐ x 5 = 30

4 x 5 = ☐

Speed calculations

Write down the answers to these calculations as quickly as you can.
See if you can finish them all in two minutes.

8 x 5 = ◯   5 x 1 = ◯

5 x 4 = ◯   7 x 5 = ◯

9 x 5 = ◯   11 x 5 = ◯

5 x 6 = ◯   5 x 3 = ◯

2 x 5 = ◯   4 x 5 = ◯

5 x 10 = ◯   5 x 9 = ◯

3 x 5 = ◯   6 x 5 = ◯

12 x 5 = ◯   5 x 7 = ◯

5 x 5 = ◯   10 x 5 = ◯

Count the dots

Use the sets of dots next to each calculation to help you count to each number in the 6x table. Write the answers in the circles.

1 x 6 = 6

2 x 6 =

3 x 6 =

4 x 6 =

5 x 6 =

6 x 6 =

7 x 6 =

8 x 6 =

9 x 6 =

10 x 6 =

11 x 6 =

12 x 6 =

Egg sixes

Count up the eggs in sixes. Follow the arrows,
and write the new total under each group.

6 → **12** → ☐ → ☐

+

☐ ← ☐ ← ☐ ← ☐

+

☐ → ☐ → ☐ → ☐

Missing numbers

Fill in the missing numbers to complete the 6x table.

$1 \times 6 = 6$

$7 \times 6 = \bigcirc$

$2 \times \bigcirc = 12$

$\bigcirc \times 6 = 48$

$\bigcirc \times 6 = 18$

$9 \times \bigcirc = 54$

$4 \times 6 = \bigcirc$

$10 \times 6 = \bigcirc$

$\bigcirc \times 6 = 30$

$11 \times 6 = \bigcirc$

$6 \times 6 = \bigcirc$

$\bigcirc \times 6 = 72$

Snowflakes

Write the number of snowflakes in each group. Then write the
total number of points in each group. (Every snowflake has six.)

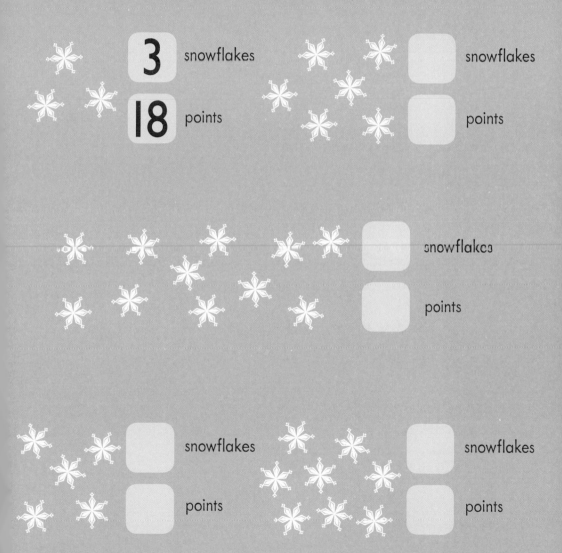

3 snowflakes

18 points

snowflakes

points

snowflakes

points

snowflakes

points

snowflakes

points

Empty boxes

Write the missing numbers in the boxes to complete these multiplications.

$6 \times \boxed{} = 42$

$10 \times 6 = \boxed{}$

$\boxed{} \times 6 = 18$

$6 \times 12 = \boxed{}$

$\boxed{} \times 6 = 12$

$6 \times \boxed{} = 36$

Number wheel

Fill in the blank sections of the number wheel so that multiplying the number in the inner ring by six gives the number in the outer ring.

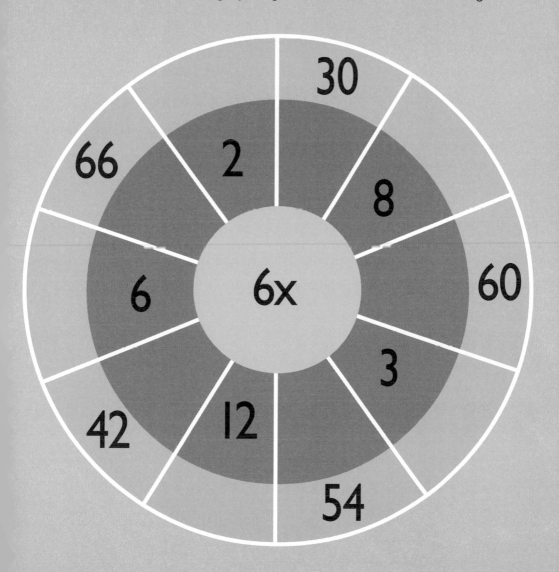

Dice dots

Change these groups of sixes into 6x table multiplication facts.

Example: ▦ ▦ ▦ ▦ = 4 x 6 = 24

= .... X .... = ...

= .... X .... = ...

= .... X .... = ...

= .... X .... = ...

= .... X .... = ...

Multiplying machines 6x

Fill in the boxes to complete all of the multiplications by six.

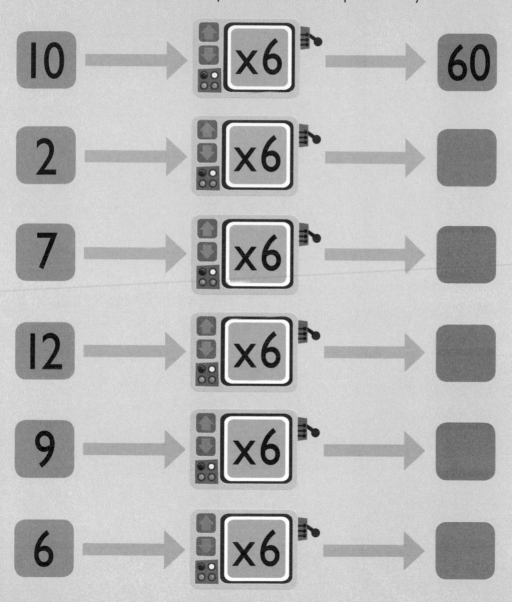

10 → x6 → 60

2 → x6 →

7 → x6 →

12 → x6 →

9 → x6 →

6 → x6 →

Word problems

Use the 6x table to solve these word problems,
and write your answers in the boxes.

There are six rockets in a box of fireworks.
How many rockets are in five boxes of fireworks?

A farmer's horse eats nine bales of hay a week.
How many bales of hay does it eat in six weeks?

An electrician has to wire up six lights in each room.
How many lights is that, if there are three rooms?

The Clark family always divides pizzas into eight slices.
How many slices is that if they order six pizzas?

At the aquarium, Sophie looked into six fish tanks.
If each tank held twelve fish, how many fish did she see?

  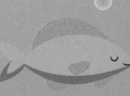

Empty boxes

Write the missing numbers in the boxes to complete these multiplications.

6 x 9 = ☐

☐ x 6 = 30

6 x ☐ = 48

☐ x 6 = 6

6 x ☐ = 24

6 x 11 = ☐

Speed calculations

Write down the answers to these calculations as quickly as you can.
See if you can finish them all in two minutes.

6 x 9 =

11 x 6 =

4 x 6 =

6 x 2 =

6 x 11 =

1 x 6 =

7 x 6 =

6 x 8 =

6 x 3 =

6 x 5 =

6 x 6 =

10 x 6 =

8 x 6 =

6 x 7 =

6 x 12 =

6 x 4 =

5 x 6 =

9 x 6 =

Count the dots

Use the sets of dots next to each calculation to help you count to each number in the 7x table. Write the answers in the circles.

1 x 7 = (7)

2 x 7 = ( )

3 x 7 = ( )

4 x 7 = ( )

5 x 7 = ( )

6 x 7 = ( )

7 x 7 = ( )

8 x 7 = ( )

9 x 7 = ( )

10 x 7 = ( )

11 x 7 = ( )

12 x 7 = ( )

Cog sevens

Count up the cogs in sevens. Follow the arrows,
and write the new total under each group.

7 → 14 → ☐ → ☐

↓ +

← ← ←

+ ↓

→ → →

Missing numbers

Fill in the missing numbers to complete the 7x table.

1 x 7 = 7   ◯ x 7 = 49

◯ x 7 = 14   8 x 7 = ◯

3 x 7 = ◯   9 x ◯ = 63

4 x ◯ = 28   10 x 7 = ◯

5 x 7 = ◯   ◯ x 7 = 77

◯ x 7 = 42   12 x 7 = ◯

Spotted bugs

Write the number of bugs in each group. Then write the total number of spots in each group. (Each bug has seven.)

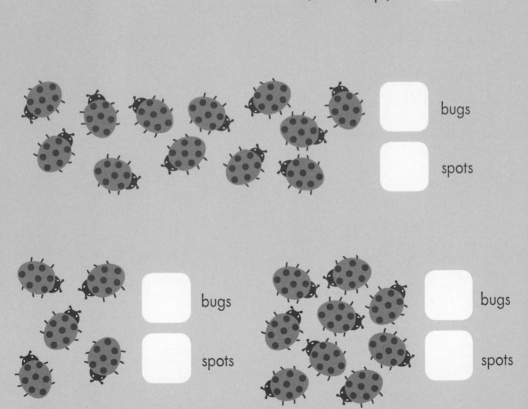

2 bugs

14 spots

bugs

spots

bugs

spots

bugs

spots

bugs

spots

Empty boxes

Write the missing numbers in the boxes to complete these multiplications.

$$\boxed{} \times 7 = 28$$

$$7 \times \boxed{} = 42$$

$$11 \times 7 = \boxed{}$$

$$7 \times \boxed{} = 63$$

$$\boxed{} \times 7 = 14$$

$$7 \times 8 = \boxed{}$$

Number wheel

Fill in the blank sections of the number wheel so that multiplying the number in the inner ring by seven gives the number in the outer ring.

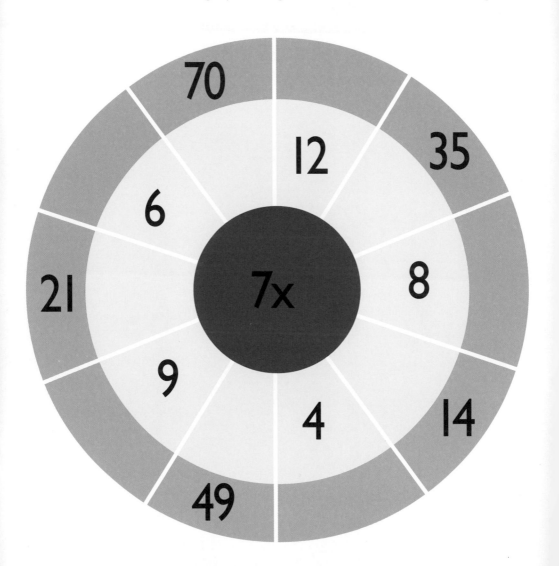

Domino dots

Change these groups of sevens into 7x table multiplication facts.

Example:

= 3 x 7 = 21

= .... x .... = ...

= .... x .... = ...

= .... x .... = ...

= .... x .... = ...

Multiplying machines

Fill in the boxes to complete all of the multiplications by seven.

5 → x7 → 35

8 → x7 →

II → x7 →

2 → x7 →

7 → x7 →

3 → x7 →

Word problems

Use the 7x table to solve these word problems,
and write your answers in the boxes.

Mr. Walsh eats three meals a day.
How many meals does he eat in a week?

Harry looks around seven exhibits in the museum.
If he spends eight minutes at each one, how long is that?

There are six erasers in a pack.
How many erasers are there in seven packs?

A business employs twelve workers in each of its offices.
If it has seven offices, how many workers is that in total?

Five oranges are needed to make a glass of fresh juice.
How many oranges are needed to make seven glasses?

Empty boxes

Write the missing numbers in the boxes to complete these multiplications.

7 x 7 = ☐

☐ x 7 = 7

7 x ☐ = 21

11 x 7 = ☐

7 x ☐ = 84

☐ x 7 = 35

Speed calculations

Write down the answers to these calculations as quickly as you can.
See if you can finish them all in two minutes.

11 x 7 =

7 x 8 =

4 x 7 =

7 x 6 =

10 x 7 =

7 x 5 =

7 x 7 =

1 x 7 =

9 x 7 =

7 x 3 =

12 x 7 =

7 x 10 =

5 x 7 =

8 x 7 =

7 x 4 =

7 x 9 =

6 x 7 =

7 x 2 =

Count the dots

Use the sets of dots next to each calculation to help you count to each number in the 8x table. Write the answers in the circles.

1 x 8 = 8

2 x 8 =

3 x 8 =

4 x 8 =

5 x 8 =

6 x 8 =

7 x 8 =

8 x 8 =

9 x 8 =

10 x 8 =

11 x 8 =

12 x 8 =

Blackbird eights

Count up the blackbirds in eights. Follow the arrows,
and write the new total under each group.

8 → **16** → ☐ → ☐

☐ ← ☐ ← ☐ ← ☐

☐ → ☐ → ☐ → ☐

Missing numbers

Fill in the missing numbers to complete the 8x table.

1 x 8 = ⬤8   ⬤ x 8 = 56

⬤ x 8 = 16   8 x ⬤ = 64

3 x 8 = ⬤   9 x 8 = ⬤

⬤ x 8 = 32   10 x 8 = ⬤

5 x ⬤ = 40   ⬤ x 8 = 88

6 x 8 = ⬤   12 x 8 = ⬤

Octopus legs

Write the number of octopuses in each group. Then write the
total number of legs in each group. (Each octopus has eight.)

 2 octopuses

 16 legs

 octopuses

 legs

 octopuses

 legs

 octopuses

 legs

 octopuses

 legs

Empty boxes

Write the missing numbers in the boxes to complete these multiplications.

☐ x 8 = 72

4 x 8 = ☐

8 x ☐ = 88

8 x 8 = ☐

8 x ☐ = 48

☐ x 8 = 8

Number wheel

Fill in the blank sections of the number wheel so that multiplying the number in the inner ring by eight gives the number in the outer ring.

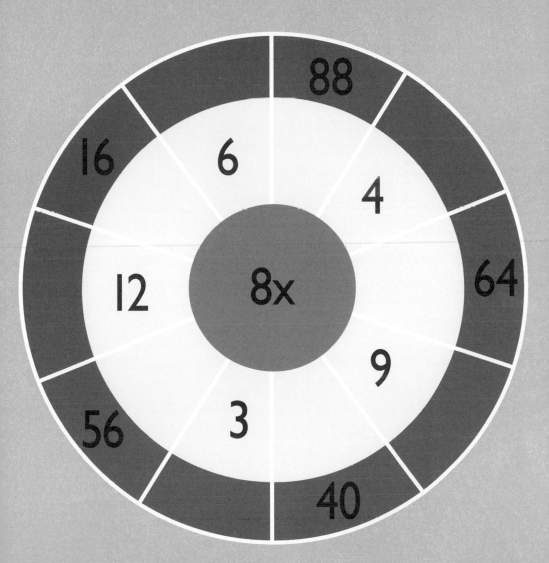

Domino dots

Change these groups of eights into 8x table multiplication facts.

Example: 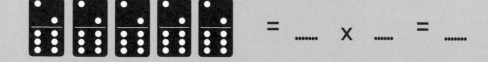 = 4 x 8 = 32

= .... x .... = ...

= .... x .... = ...

= .... x .... = ...

= .... x .... = ...

Multiplying machines

Fill in the boxes to complete all of the multiplications by eight.

3 → x8 → 24

9 → x8 →

5 → x8 →

12 → x8 →

7 → x8 →

10 → x8 →

Word problems

Use the 8x table to solve these word problems,
and write your answers in the boxes.

A tarantula has eight legs.
How many legs are there on six tarantulas?

There is enough room for eight people to sit on a bench.
How many people can sit on twelve benches?

Faye buys her two sisters eight presents each.
How many presents does she buy in total?

Uncle Mike bought five boxes of golf balls.
If each box contains eight, how many golf balls is that?

A talking parrot will cost a pirate captain seven doubloons.
How many doubloons would eight talking parrots cost him?

Empty boxes

Write the missing numbers in the boxes to complete these multiplications.

$8 \times \boxed{} = 24$

$8 \times 7 = \boxed{}$

$\boxed{} \times 8 = 40$

$8 \times \boxed{} = 96$

$10 \times 8 = \boxed{}$

$\boxed{} \times 8 = 16$

Speed calculations

Write down the answers to these calculations as quickly as you can.
See if you can finish them all in two minutes.

6 x 8 =   2 x 8 =

8 x 10 =   8 x 4 =

3 x 8 =   11 x 8 =

8 x 2 =   7 x 8 =

8 x 12 =   8 x 3 =

5 x 8 =   8 x 6 =

8 x 9 =   12 x 8 =

1 x 8 =   8 x 8 =

8 x 7 =   8 x 5 =

Count the dots

Use the sets of dots next to each calculation to help you count to each number in the 9x table. Write the answers in the circles.

1 x 9 = (9)

2 x 9 = ( )

3 x 9 = ( )

4 x 9 = ( )

5 x 9 = ( )

6 x 9 = ( )

7 x 9 = ( )

8 x 9 = ( )

9 x 9 = ( )

10 x 9 = ( )

11 x 9 = ( )

12 x 9 = ( )

Strawberry nines

Count up the strawberries in nines. Follow the arrows,
and write the new total under each group.

9 → **18** → ☐ → ☐

+

☐ ← ☐ ← ☐ ← ☐

+

☐ → ☐ → ☐ → ☐

Missing numbers

9x

Fill in the missing numbers to complete the 9x table.

$1 \times 9 = 9$

$7 \times 9 = \bigcirc$

$\bigcirc \times 9 = 18$

$\bigcirc \times 9 = 72$

$3 \times \bigcirc = 27$

$9 \times 9 = \bigcirc$

$4 \times 9 = \bigcirc$

$10 \times \bigcirc = 90$

$5 \times 9 = \bigcirc$

$11 \times 9 = \bigcirc$

$\bigcirc \times 9 = 54$

$\bigcirc \times 9 = 108$

House windows

Write the number of houses in each group. Then write the total number of windows in each group. (Each house has nine.)

4 houses

36 windows

houses

windows

houses

windows

houses

windows

houses

windows

Empty boxes

Write the missing numbers in the boxes to complete these multiplications.

$9 \times 5 = \boxed{}$

$\boxed{} \times 9 = 18$

$9 \times \boxed{} = 81$

$\boxed{} \times 9 = 108$

$3 \times 9 = \boxed{}$

$9 \times \boxed{} = 72$

Number wheel

Fill in the blank sections of the number wheel so that multiplying the number in the inner ring by nine gives the number in the outer ring.

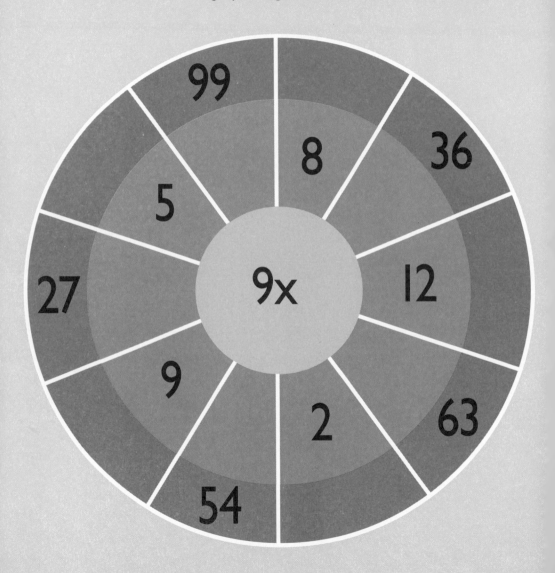

Domino dots

Change these groups of nines into 9x table multiplication facts.

Example:

= 3 x 9 = 27

= .... x .... = ...

= .... x .... = ...

= .... x .... = ...

= .... x .... = ...

Multiplying machines

Fill in the boxes to complete all of the multiplications by nine.

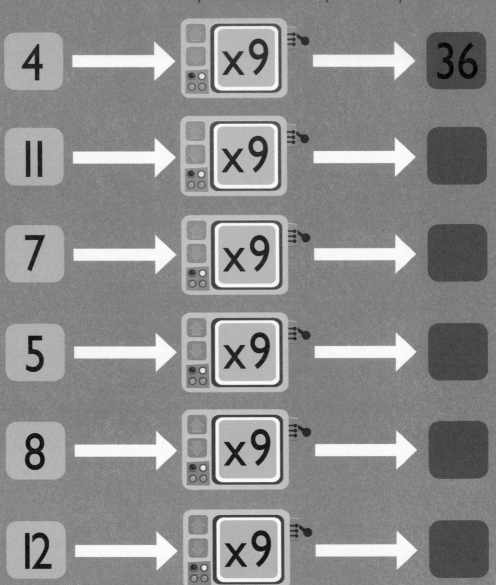

4 → x9 → 36

11 → x9 →

7 → x9 →

5 → x9 →

8 → x9 →

12 → x9 →

Word problems

Use the 9x table to solve these word problems,
and write your answers in the boxes.

Hayley goes to see nine new movies in a month.
If each film lasts two hours, how many hours is that in total?

Twelve Dalmatians give birth to nine puppies each.
How many Dalmatian puppies is that altogether?

Peter has a party and cooks five sausage rolls for each guest.
How many sausage rolls does he cook If he has nine guests?

A high-rise building contains nine luxury apartments.
If three people live in each one, how many live in the building?

Each boat at the lake can hold eight people.
How many people can nine boats hold?

Empty boxes

Write the missing numbers in the boxes to complete these multiplications.

$9 \times \boxed{} = 99$

$4 \times 9 = \boxed{}$

$\boxed{} \times 9 = 63$

$9 \times \boxed{} = 45$

$\boxed{} \times 9 = 90$

$9 \times 6 = \boxed{}$

Speed calculations

9x

Write down the answers to these calculations as quickly as you can.
See if you can finish them all in two minutes.

4 x 9 =

9 x 12 =

7 x 9 =

9 x 3 =

6 x 9 =

9 x 9 =

12 x 9 =

9 x 10 =

2 x 9 =

9 x 6 =

1 x 9 =

8 x 9 =

9 x 5 =

9 x 2 =

10 x 9 =

3 x 9 =

9 x 7 =

11 x 9 =

Count the dots

Use the sets of dots next to each calculation to help you count to
each number in the 10x table. Write the answers in the circles.

1 x 10 = 10

2 x 10 =

3 x 10 =

4 x 10 =

5 x 10 =

6 x 10 =

7 x 10 =

8 x 10 =

9 x 10 =

10 x 10 =

11 x 10 =

12 x 10 =

Light bulbs

Count up the light bulbs in tens. Follow the arrows,
and write the new total under each group.

10 → **20** → ☐ → ☐ +

+ ☐ ← ☐ ← ☐ ← ☐ +

+ ☐ → ☐ → ☐ → ☐

Missing numbers

10x

Fill in the missing numbers to complete the 10x table.

1 x 10 = 10

7 x 10 = ⬤

2 x ⬤ = 20

⬤ x 10 = 80

⬤ x 10 = 30

9 x ⬤ = 90

4 x 10 = ⬤

10 x 10 = ⬤

⬤ x 10 = 50

11 x 10 = ⬤

6 x 10 = ⬤

⬤ x 10 = 120

Birthday candles

Write the number of cakes in each group. Then write the total
number of candles in each group. (Each cake has ten.)

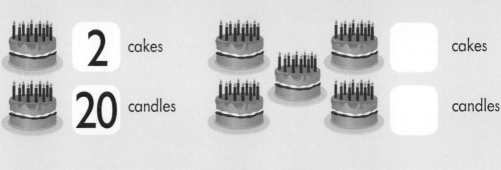

2 cakes

20 candles

cakes

candles

cakes

candles

cakes

candles

cakes

candles

Empty boxes

Write the missing numbers in the boxes to complete these multiplications.

$$7 \times 10 = \boxed{}$$

$$10 \times \boxed{} = 20$$

$$\boxed{} \times 10 = 110$$

$$10 \times \boxed{} = 10$$

$$\boxed{} \times 10 = 80$$

$$10 \times 10 = \boxed{}$$

Number wheel

Fill in the blank sections of the number wheel so that multiplying the number in the inner ring by ten gives the number in the outer ring.

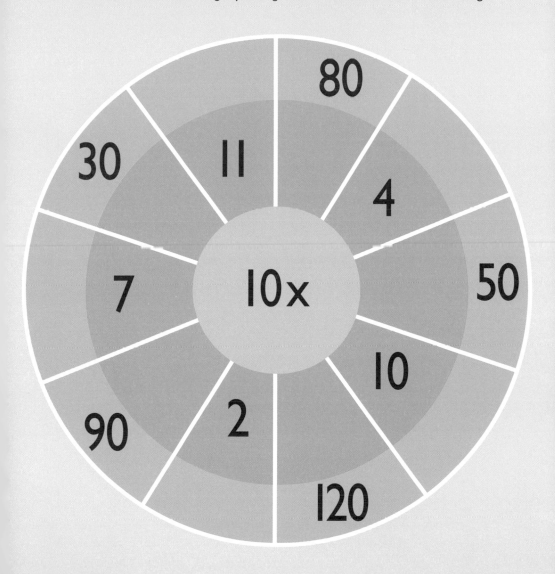

Domino dots

10x

Change these groups of tens into 10x table multiplication facts.

Example: = 4 x 10 = 40

= .... x .... = ...

= .... x .... = ...

= .... x .... = ...

= .... x .... = ...

Multiplying machines

10x

Fill in the boxes to complete all of the multiplications by ten.

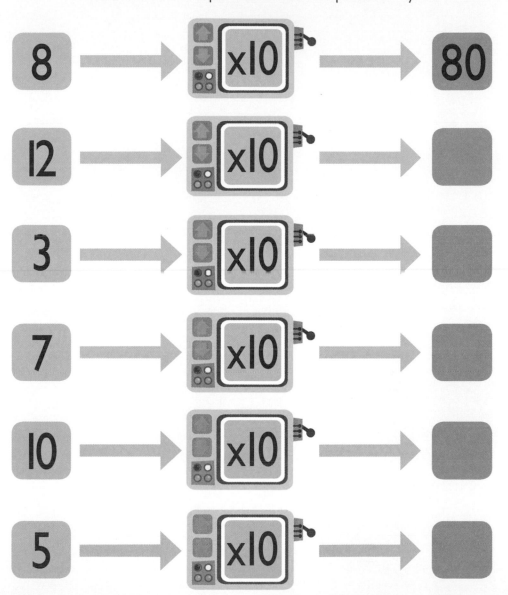

Word problems

Use the 10x table to solve these word problems,
and write your answers in the boxes.

Jane has made ten pitchers of lemonade for her party.
How many glasses is that if one pitcher fills five glasses?

Simon uses ten nails for each board in his treehouse.
How many nails does he need for twelve boards?

Theo takes the family dog on ten walks a week.
How many times will he walk the dog in three weeks?

A small plane has enough seats for ten passengers.
How many passengers can ride in seven small planes?

A crab has ten legs.
How many legs do ten crabs have?

Empty boxes

Write the missing numbers in the boxes to complete these multiplications.

$\boxed{} \times 10 = 40$

$10 \times 6 = \boxed{}$

$10 \times \boxed{} = 100$

$\boxed{} \times 10 = 30$

$10 \times 12 = \boxed{}$

$10 \times \boxed{} = 90$

Speed calculations

Write down the answers to these calculations as quickly as you can.
See if you can finish them all in two minutes.

5 x 10 = ◯   10 x 1 = ◯

10 x 8 = ◯   7 x 10 = ◯

3 x 10 = ◯   10 x 3 = ◯

12 x 10 = ◯   11 x 10 = ◯

10 x 6 = ◯   8 x 10 = ◯

4 x 10 = ◯   10 x 5 = ◯

10 x 10 = ◯   6 x 10 = ◯

10 x 2 = ◯   10 x 12 = ◯

9 x 10 = ◯   10 x 4 = ◯

Count the dots

Use the sets of dots next to each calculation to help you count to
each number in the 11x table. Write the answers in the circles.

1 x 11 = 11

2 x 11 =

3 x 11 =

4 x 11 =

5 x 11 =

6 x 11 =

7 x 11 =

8 x 11 =

9 x 11 =

10 x 11 =

11 x 11 =

12 x 11 =

Apple elevens

Count up the apples in elevens. Follow the arrows,
and write the new total under each group.

11 + + + +

11 → **22** → → →

+ + + +

← ← ←

+

+ + + +

→ → → →

Missing numbers

Fill in the missing numbers to complete the 11x table.

1 x 11 = 11   ◯ x 11 = 77

◯ x 11 = 22   8 x 11 = ◯

3 x 11 = ◯   9 x ◯ = 99

4 x ◯ = 44   10 x 11 = ◯

5 x 11 = ◯   ◯ x 11 = 121

◯ x 11 = 66   12 x 11 = ◯

Plant leaves

Write the number of plants in each group. Then write the total
number of leaves in each group. (Each plant has eleven.)

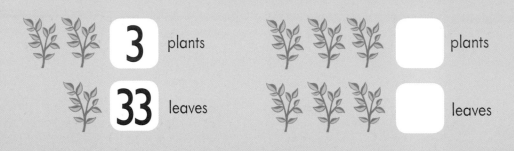

3 plants

33 leaves

plants

leaves

plants

leaves

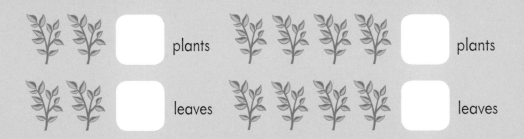

plants

leaves

plants

leaves

Empty boxes

Write the missing numbers in the boxes to complete these multiplications.

11 x 4 = ☐

☐ x 11 = 99

11 x ☐ = 66

☐ x 11 = 121

11 x ☐ = 22

10 x 11 = ☐

Number wheel

Fill in the blank sections of the number wheel so that multiplying the number in the inner ring by eleven gives the number in the outer ring.

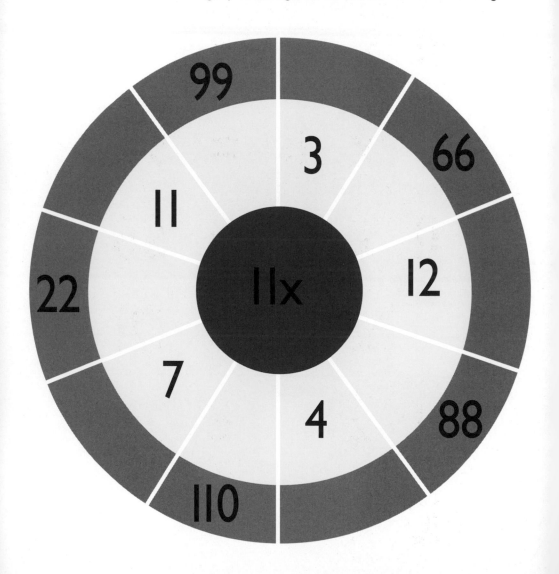

Domino dots

Change these groups of elevens into 11x table multiplication facts.

Example:

= 3 x 11 = 33

= .... x .... = ...

= .... x .... = ...

= .... x .... = ...

= .... x .... = ...

Multiplying machines

Fill in the boxes to complete all of the multiplications by eleven.

6 ➡️ x11 ➡️ 66

12 ➡️ x11 ➡️

5 ➡️ x11 ➡️

2 ➡️ x11 ➡️

8 ➡️ x11 ➡️

11 ➡️ x11 ➡️

Word problems

Use the 11x table to solve these word problems,
and write your answers in the boxes.

Amy gives out eleven party bags at the end of her birthday.
How many toys does she give out if each bag contains three?

There are eleven grapes in a bunch.
How many grapes are there in twelve bunches?

Liam finishes two books every week.
How many books does he finish in eleven weeks?

It takes Shelly five minutes to draw an elephant.
How long would it take her to draw eleven elephants?

A gardener plants eleven flowers in every flowerbed.
If there are nine flowerbeds, how many flowers does he plant?

Empty boxes

Write the missing numbers in the boxes to complete these multiplications.

11 x 7 = ☐

☐ x 11 = 55

11 x ☐ = 132

☐ x 11 = 33

11 x ☐ = 88

10 x 11 = ☐

Speed calculations

Write down the answers to these calculations as quickly as you can.
See if you can finish them all in two minutes.

2 x 11 =

11 x 9 =

5 x 11 =

11 x 10 =

7 x 11 =

3 x 11 =

11 x 8 =

11 x 11 =

6 x 11 =

10 x 11 =

11 x 4 =

8 x 11 =

11 x 12 =

1 x 11 =

11 x 5 =

9 x 11 =

11 x 7 =

12 x 11 =

Count the dots

Use the sets of dots next to each calculation to help you count to each number in the 12x table. Write the answers in the circles.

1 x 12 = (12)

2 x 12 = (   )

3 x 12 = (   )

4 x 12 = (   )

5 x 12 = (   )

6 x 12 = (   )

7 x 12 = (   )

8 x 12 = (   )

9 x 12 = (   )

10 x 12 = (   )

11 x 12 = (   )

12 x 12 = (   )

Rockets

12x

Count up the rockets in twelves. Follow the arrows,
and write the new total under each group.

12 → **24** → ☐ → ☐

☐ ← ☐ ← ☐ ← ☐

☐ → ☐ → ☐ → ☐

Missing numbers

12x

Fill in the missing numbers to complete the 12x table.

1 x 12 = 12

◯ x 12 = 84

◯ x 12 = 24

8 x ◯ = 96

3 x 12 = ◯

9 x 12 = ◯

◯ x 12 = 48

10 x 12 = ◯

5 x ◯ = 60

◯ x 12 = 132

6 x 12 = ◯

12 x 12 = ◯

Fruit swirls

Write the number of jars in each group. Then write the total
number of fruit swirls in each group. (Each jar contains twelve.)

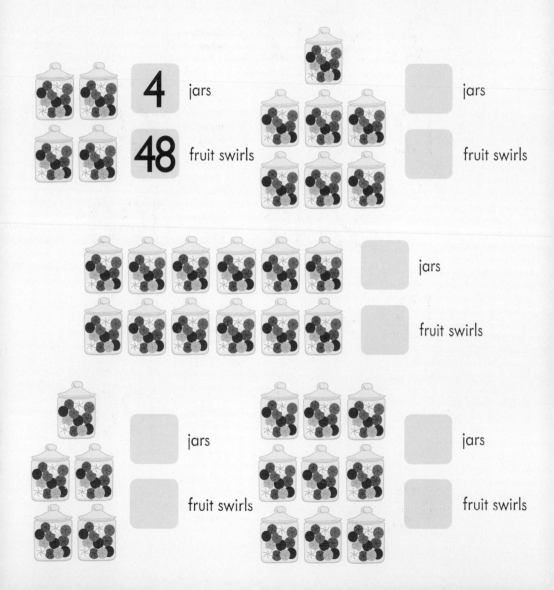

4 jars

48 fruit swirls

jars

fruit swirls

jars

fruit swirls

jars

fruit swirls

jars

fruit swirls

Empty boxes

Write the missing numbers in the boxes to complete these multiplications.

$2 \times 12 = \boxed{}$

$12 \times \boxed{} = 60$

$\boxed{} \times 12 = 108$

$12 \times \boxed{} = 48$

$\boxed{} \times 12 = 120$

$12 \times 7 = \boxed{}$

Number wheel

Fill in the blank sections of the number wheel so that multiplying the number in the inner ring by twelve gives the number in the outer ring.

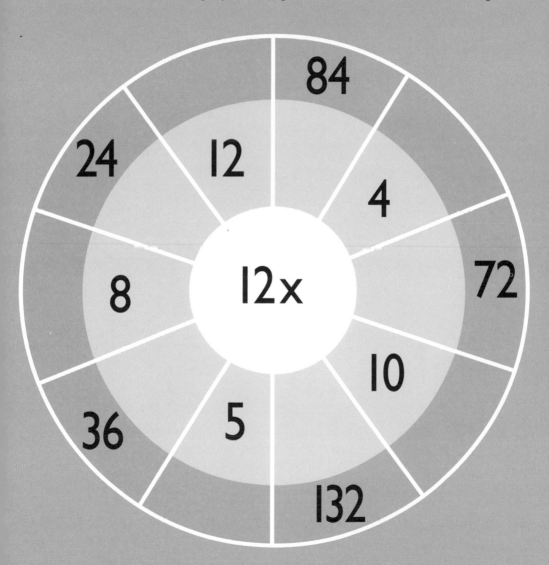

Domino dots

Change these groups of twelves into 12x table multiplication facts.

Example: = 2 x 12 = 24

= .... x .... = ...

= .... x .... = ...

= .... x .... = ...

= .... x .... = ...

Multiplying machines

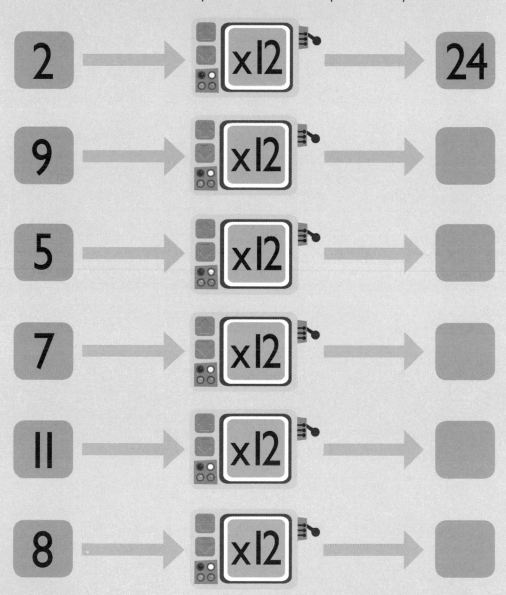

12x

Fill in the boxes to complete all of the multiplications by twelve.

2 → x12 → 24

9 → x12 →

5 → x12 →

7 → x12 →

11 → x12 →

8 → x12 →

Word problems

Use the 12x table to solve these word problems,
and write your answers in the boxes.

A box of chocolates has twelve chocolates on each layer.
If the box has three layers, how many chocolates are in it?

Lucy has nine full racks of DVDs in her bedroom.
If each rack holds twelve DVDs, how many does she own?

A clown can make a balloon animal in two minutes.
How long would he take to make twelve balloon animals?

A roller coaster at an amusement park has twelve cars.
If each car holds twelve people, how many can ride it at once?

In a game of cards, five friends are dealt twelve cards each.
How many cards have been dealt altogether?

Empty boxes

Write the missing numbers in the boxes to complete these multiplications.

$\boxed{} \times 12 = 132$

$12 \times 8 = \boxed{}$

$12 \times \boxed{} = 36$

$\boxed{} \times 12 = 84$

$12 \times \boxed{} = 72$

$12 \times 12 = \boxed{}$

Speed calculations

Write down the answers to these calculations as quickly as you can.
See if you can finish them all in two minutes.

5 x 12 =   12 x 7 =

12 x 8 =   12 x 10 =

2 x 12 =   1 x 12 =

7 x 12 =   12 x 6 =

12 x 12 =   12 x 11 =

10 x 12 =   4 x 12 =

12 x 3 =   12 x 2 =

6 x 12 =   12 x 5 =

12 x 4 =   9 x 12 =

Square numbers

In the calculations below, the numbers are being squared (multiplied by themselves). Write their answers, called square numbers, in the boxes.

1 x 1 =

2 x 2 =

3 x 3 =

4 x 4 =

5 x 5 =

6 x 6 =

7 x 7 =

8 x 8 =

9 x 9 =

10 x 10 =

11 x 11 =

12 x 12 =

Same answers

Write the answers to each calculation below, then fill in the missing number in the second calculation so it equals the same.

Example: $2 \times 2 = 4 = 1 \times 4$

$4 \times 12 = \boxed{} = \boxed{} \times 6$

$9 \times 1 = \boxed{} = 3 \times \boxed{}$

$5 \times 8 = \boxed{} = \boxed{} \times 10$

$12 \times 3 = \boxed{} = 4 \times \boxed{}$

$8 \times 9 = \boxed{} = \boxed{} \times 6$

Word problems

Use the correct tables to solve each of these word problems, and write your answers in the boxes.

Each of a company's planes has eight crew members. How many crew members are there on five planes?

A volcano erupts every six years. How many times does it erupt in 54 years?

A crew of seven pirates has 49 gold coins to share. How many gold coins will each pirate get?

Bella's café sells five muffins an hour. How many muffins does it sell in three hours?

144 fireworks go off in a twelve-minute display. How many fireworks go off each minute?

Multiplying machines

Fill in the boxes to complete all of the multiplications below.

4 ➞ x6 ➞ 24

9 ➞ x3 ➞

12 ➞ x11 ➞

8 ➞ x7 ➞

3 ➞ x5 ➞

10 ➞ x2 ➞

Speed calculations

Write down the answers to these calculations as quickly as you can.
See if you can finish them all in three minutes.

4 x 7 = ⬭   3 x 3 = ⬭

9 x 3 = ⬭   5 x 11 = ⬭

8 x 5 = ⬭   10 x 7 = ⬭

12 x 6 = ⬭   4 x 2 = ⬭

2 x 10 = ⬭   5 x 9 = ⬭

11 x 12 = ⬭   6 x 8 = ⬭

9 x 8 = ⬭   2 x 12 = ⬭

5 x 3 = ⬭   9 x 9 = ⬭

7 x 6 = ⬭   5 x 4 = ⬭

Speed calculations

Write down the answers to these calculations as quickly as you can.
See if you can finish them all in three minutes.

6 x 10 =   4 x 3 =

7 x 4 =   2 x 5 =

9 x 5 =   7 x 7 =

3 x 12 =   8 x 9 =

6 x 6 =   12 x 2 =

5 x 8 =   3 x 6 =

2 x 11 =   7 x 2 =

10 x 5 =   9 x 4 =

12 x 12 =   6 x 11 =

Speed calculations

Write down the answers to these calculations as quickly as you can.
See if you can finish them all in three minutes.

5 x 5 =

12 x 3 =

8 x 6 =

2 x 4 =

10 x 7 =

11 x 11 =

9 x 12 =

4 x 8 =

3 x 7 =

8 x 9 =

5 x 10 =

10 x 2 =

7 x 12 =

4 x 4 =

3 x 9 =

11 x 8 =

6 x 7 =

5 x 4 =

Speed calculations

Write down the answers to these calculations as quickly as you can.
See if you can finish them all in three minutes.

5 x 8 =

7 x 3 =

4 x 10 =

10 x 10 =

9 x 2 =

5 x 4 =

3 x 6 =

8 x 12 =

7 x 7 =

9 x 7 =

12 x 5 =

4 x 3 =

8 x 3 =

6 x 6 =

11 x 12 =

9 x 5 =

6 x 9 =

3 x 12 =

Multiplying machines

Fill in the boxes to complete all of the multiplications below.

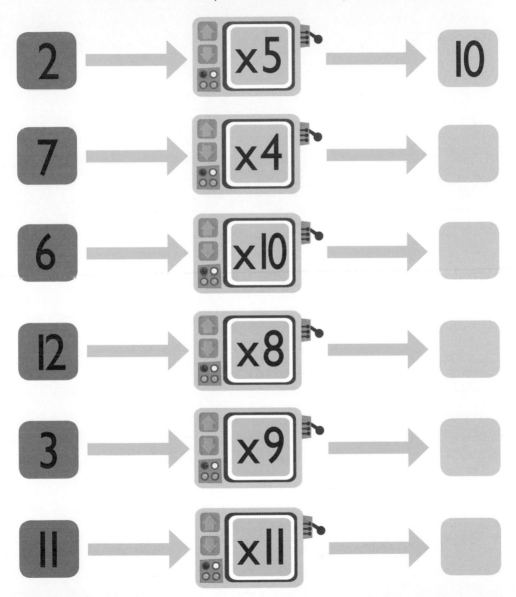

2 → x5 → 10

7 → x4 →

6 → x10 →

12 → x8 →

3 → x9 →

11 → x11 →

Speed calculations

Write down the answers to these calculations as quickly as you can.
See if you can finish them all in three minutes.

5 x 2 =

9 x 10 =

12 x 3 =

4 x 4 =

8 x 7 =

6 x 5 =

9 x 3 =

10 x 6 =

2 x 2 =

8 x 11 =

4 x 12 =

3 x 5 =

6 x 7 =

9 x 8 =

11 x 4 =

8 x 2 =

12 x 9 =

4 x 6 =

Word problems

Use the correct tables to solve each of these word problems, and write your answers in the boxes.

Millie sews eight buttons onto each shirt she makes. How many buttons does she need for twelve shirts?

Sonny's Circus gives nine performances a week. How many perfomances does it give in six weeks?

A rabbit warren has eight equal-size burrows. How many of its 64 rabbits live in each burrow?

A pirate fleet of twelve ships has 132 cannons in total. How many cannons does each ship have?

A go-kart takes four minutes to do a lap. How many minutes will it take to do seven laps?

Same answers

Write the answers to each calculation below, then fill in the
missing number in the second calculation so it equals the same.

Example: $1 \times 12 = 12 = 3 \times 4$

$8 \times 3 = \boxed{} = 6 \times \boxed{}$

$4 \times 4 = \boxed{} = \boxed{} \times 2$

$5 \times 6 = \boxed{} = 3 \times \boxed{}$

$9 \times 4 = \boxed{} = \boxed{} \times 6$

$10 \times 1 = \boxed{} = 5 \times \boxed{}$

Speed calculations

Write down the answers to these calculations as quickly as you can.
See if you can finish them all in three minutes.

4 x 8 = ⬤   3 x 7 = ⬤

5 x 3 = ⬤   6 x 4 = ⬤

12 x 11 = ⬤   8 x 8 = ⬤

9 x 6 = ⬤   2 x 9 = ⬤

7 x 8 = ⬤   5 x 12 = ⬤

10 x 10 = ⬤   8 x 6 = ⬤

6 x 2 = ⬤   7 x 5 = ⬤

5 x 5 = ⬤   3 x 11 = ⬤

4 x 12 = ⬤   10 x 4 = ⬤

Word problems

Use the correct tables to solve each of these word problems, and write your answers in the boxes.

A train stops at the station every seven minutes.
How many trains stop there in 56 minutes?

A chef uses six tomatoes in his salad.
How many salads can he make with 36 tomatoes?

Lucy, Tom and Nicola share twelve cookies equally.
How many cookies each is that?

There are 22 socks drying on the line.
How many pairs is that?

Five people can sleep in a tent.
How many tents are needed for 45 people?

Speed calculations

Write down the answers to these calculations as quickly as you can.
See if you can finish them all in three minutes.

2 x 6 =

9 x 3 =

12 x 7 =

5 x 4 =

8 x 9 =

3 x 6 =

4 x 2 =

10 x 3 =

8 x 5 =

7 x 7 =

6 x 12 =

10 x 5 =

2 x 8 =

9 x 11 =

12 x 4 =

6 x 8 =

12 x 12 =

3 x 7 =

Multiplying machines

Fill in the boxes to complete all of the multiplications below.

10 → x6 → 60

3 → x8 →

7 → x5 →

8 → x9 →

11 → x2 →

6 → x12 →

Same answers

Write the answers to each calculation below, then fill in the missing number in the second calculation so it equals the same.

Example: 6 x 6 = 36 = 4 x 9

2 x 10 = = 5 x

3 x 8 = = 12 x

6 x 2 = = 3 x

1 x 8 = = x 2

12 x 5 = = 10 x

Word problems

Use the correct tables to solve each of these word problems, and write your answers in the boxes.

121 schoolchildren are divided into eleven equal groups. How many children are in each group?

Six dogs have nine puppies each. How many puppies is that altogether?

It takes Jake ten minutes to polish a pair of shoes. How long would it take him to polish seven pairs?

Anita plays badminton five times each month. How many times does she play in a year?

A jellyfish has ten tentacles. How many tentacles do four jellyfish have?

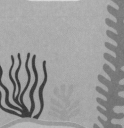

Speed calculations

Write down the answers to these calculations as quickly as you can.
See if you can finish them all in three minutes.

2 x 7 = ◯ 3 x 4 = ◯

4 x 9 = ◯ 8 x 12 = ◯

10 x 8 = ◯ 4 x 6 = ◯

6 x 3 = ◯ 7 x 11 = ◯

9 x 12 = ◯ 3 x 2 = ◯

5 x 5 = ◯ 6 x 9 = ◯

8 x 4 = ◯ 5 x 7 = ◯

11 x 10 = ◯ 3 x 8 = ◯

9 x 7 = ◯ 11 x 2 = ◯

Speed calculations

Write down the answers to these calculations as quickly as you can.
See if you can finish them all in three minutes.

5 x 6 = ⬤   3 x 9 = ⬤

8 x 3 = ⬤   11 x 11 = ⬤

4 x 11 = ⬤   6 x 12 = ⬤

7 x 2 = ⬤   2 x 3 = ⬤

10 x 12 = ⬤   11 x 5 = ⬤

9 x 4 = ⬤   8 x 10 = ⬤

2 x 8 = ⬤   4 x 4 = ⬤

4 x 5 = ⬤   7 x 9 = ⬤

6 x 7 = ⬤   12 x 8 = ⬤

Word problems

Use the correct tables to solve each of these word problems, and write your answers in the boxes.

A tractor ride takes nine people around the farm. If there are 108 customers, how many rides is that?

A tank can hold eight gallons of water. How many tanks are needed to hold 56 gallons?

Horace has 121 pineapples and eleven crates. How many pineapples is that per crate?

Four friends each eat two hot dogs. How many hot dogs is that altogether?

A frog catches a fly every five minutes. How many flies will it catch in 25 minutes?

Speed calculations

Write down the answers to these calculations as quickly as you can.
See if you can finish them all in three minutes.

8 x 8 =

3 x 9 =

4 x 6 =

12 x 11 =

7 x 5 =

8 x 9 =

10 x 10 =

2 x 6 =

6 x 7 =

11 x 4 =

9 x 2 =

5 x 5 =

10 x 6 =

7 x 8 =

4 x 9 =

8 x 5 =

12 x 7 =

9 x 9 =

Word problems

Use the correct tables to solve each of these word problems, and write your answers in the boxes.

Each house on a street has five windows.
How many windows are there on twelve houses?

Seven monkeys share 28 bananas between them.
How many bananas does each monkey eat?

Every hour, nine people walk their dog in the park.
How many dog walkers is that in three hours?

A can of paint is enough to paint eight fence panels.
How many cans are needed to paint 48 panels?

Helga the hen lays six eggs a week.
How many weeks does she take to lay 66 eggs?

Multiplication grid

Finish filling in the multiplication grid below. Each square's number is the product of multiplying the number at the top of that column by the number at the start of that row.

X	1	2	3	4	5	6	7	8	9	10	11	12
1								8				
2				10								
3								27				
4			12									
5	5											
6										60		
7				35								
8		16										
9						63						
10											110	
11			33									
12					72							

Speed calculations

Write down the answers to these calculations as quickly as you can.
See if you can finish them all in three minutes.

12 x 5 =   2 x 8 =

7 x 3 =   4 x 5 =

6 x 9 =   10 x 11 =

2 x 4 =   6 x 6 =

11 x 8 =   9 x 2 =

5 x 7 =   4 x 10 =

8 x 6 =   7 x 12 =

12 x 4 =   5 x 8 =

10 x 9 =   11 x 11 =

Speed calculations

Write down the answers to these calculations as quickly as you can.
See if you can finish them all in three minutes.

3 x 6 =

7 x 8 =

12 x 5 =

4 x 9 =

11 x 2 =

10 x 7 =

5 x 4 =

2 x 8 =

6 x 9 =

8 x 4 =

5 x 7 =

3 x 3 =

12 x 12 =

9 x 8 =

5 x 11 =

2 x 7 =

10 x 10 =

4 x 12 =

Speed calculations

Write down the answers to these calculations as quickly as you can.
See if you can finish them all in three minutes.

8 x 4 =

11 x 5 =

2 x 9 =

7 x 6 =

12 x 3 =

5 x 8 =

6 x 10 =

9 x 12 =

3 x 4 =

9 x 7 =

5 x 2 =

4 x 6 =

11 x 8 =

10 x 9 =

12 x 5 =

3 x 7 =

6 x 2 =

8 x 8 =

Multiplying machines

Fill in the boxes to complete all of the multiplications below.

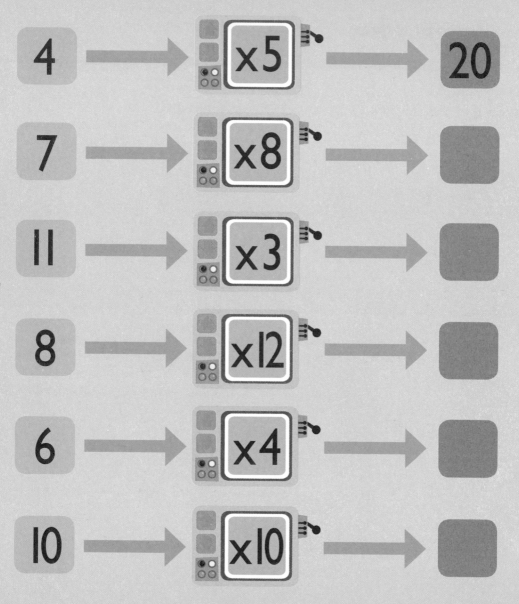

4 → x5 → 20

7 → x8 →

11 → x3 →

8 → x12 →

6 → x4 →

10 → x10 →

Top tips

You can use the tricks on this page to help you crack each times table.

2x table

Every even number is in the 2x table.

For numbers in the 2x table, just double the number you're multiplying by.

Remember "twice" means "two times".

3x table

Use the 2x table, then add the number you're multiplying by to the answer. So for 6×3, do $6 \times 2 = 12$, then $12 + 6 = 18$.

4x table

Try using the 2x table and then doubling the answer: $8 \times 2 = 16$, so $8 \times 4 = 32$.

5x table

Every number in this table ends in 0 or 5.

Try using the 10x table and then halving the answer. So for 8×5, do $8 \times 10 = 80$, then $80 \div 2 = 40$.

6x table

Try using the 3x table and then doubling the answer: $7 \times 3 = 21$, so $7 \times 6 = 42$.

7x table

Learn some 'landmarks,' like $8 \times 7 = 56$, that you can work backwards or forwards from.

8x table

Try using the 4x table and then doubling the answer: $6 \times 4 = 24$, so $6 \times 8 = 48$.

9x table

The first ten numbers in this table have digits that add up to 9. So, in 27, $2 + 7 = 9$. The first number of the answer is always one less than the number you're multiplying by ($\underline{3} \times 9 = \underline{2}7$), so the second number is just what you have to add to make 9.

Try using the 10x table and then subtracting the number you're multiplying by. So for 3×9, do $3 \times 10 = 30$, then $30 - 3 = 27$.

10x table

For numbers in the 10x table, just add a zero to the number you're multiplying by.

11x table

In the first 9 numbers of this table, both digits are the same as the number you're multiplying by. For example $5 \times 11 = 55$.

12x table

Try using the 6x table and then doubling the answer: $9 \times 6 = 54$, so $9 \times 12 = 108$.

Try using the 2x and 10x tables and adding the answers together. So for 9×12, do $9 \times 10 = 90$, then $9 \times 2 = 18$. $90 + 18 = 108$.

Top tips

Multiplying means...

There are three ways to think of multiplication.

It is counting in groups: adding on several lots of the same number or amount. So, for 3 x 5, this means adding three sets of five (5 + 5 + 5).

You can picture multiplication as an array: for example 3 x 5 stickers can be three rows of stickers with five stickers in each row.

Multiplication also means scaling. This is making something a number of times bigger or smaller, such as three times as heavy or five times as long.

Turn the tables

Multiplying two numbers always gives the same answer whichever way around you do it. For example, 3 x 5 and 5 x 3 both equal 15.
So, if you find one table tricky, you can always use another to help you. If you don't know what 10 x 11 is, you can think of it as 11 x 10 instead. Just add a zero to 11 and you've got 110.

Splitting multiplications

If a multiplication seems too tricky, you can split it up into two parts to make it easier and then add the two answers together afterwards. For example, 11 x 11 might sound hard. So, first you could do 11 x 10 instead, which gives you 110. Now just add 11 (which is 11 x 1) to your answer and you get 121.

Landmarks

10 times a number is easy, and 5 times a number will be half that. If you know these 'landmarks', you can count forward or back from them to do trickier multiplications.

For example, 6 x 7. If you know 5 x 7 = 35, you can just add 7 to that to get 42.

Multiples

If a number is a multiple of another number, it means it can be divided cleanly by that number. Therefore any number in the 3x table can be described as a multiple of 3.

It's useful to know that because 6, 9 and 12 can all be divided cleanly by 3, any number in the 6x, 9x and 12x tables will also be a multiple of 3.

Square numbers

A square number is the product of multiplying a number by itself. For example, 7 x 7 = 49, so 49 is a square number.

Prime numbers

A prime number is a number that can only be divided cleanly by itself and 1. Therefore a prime number will never appear as the answer in any other number's times table.

List of tables

1x table

1 x 1 = 1
2 x 1 = 2
3 x 1 = 3
4 x 1 = 4
5 x 1 = 5
6 x 1 = 6
7 x 1 = 7
8 x 1 = 8
9 x 1 = 9
10 x 1 = 10
11 x 1 = 11
12 x 1 = 12

2x table

1 x 2 = 2
2 x 2 = 4
3 x 2 = 6
4 x 2 = 8
5 x 2 = 10
6 x 2 = 12
7 x 2 = 14
8 x 2 = 16
9 x 2 = 18
10 x 2 = 20
11 x 2 = 22
12 x 2 = 24

3x table

1 x 3 = 3
2 x 3 = 6
3 x 3 = 9
4 x 3 = 12
5 x 3 = 15
6 x 3 = 18
7 x 3 = 21
8 x 3 = 24
9 x 3 = 27
10 x 3 = 30
11 x 3 = 33
12 x 3 = 36

4x table

1 x 4 = 4
2 x 4 = 8
3 x 4 = 12
4 x 4 = 16
5 x 4 = 20
6 x 4 = 24
7 x 4 = 28
8 x 4 = 32
9 x 4 = 36
10 x 4 = 40
11 x 4 = 44
12 x 4 = 48

5x table

1 x 5 = 5
2 x 5 = 10
3 x 5 = 15
4 x 5 = 20
5 x 5 = 25
6 x 5 = 30
7 x 5 = 35
8 x 5 = 40
9 x 5 = 45
10 x 5 = 50
11 x 5 = 55
12 x 5 = 60

6x table

1 x 6 = 6
2 x 6 = 12
3 x 6 = 18
4 x 6 = 24
5 x 6 = 30
6 x 6 = 36
7 x 6 = 42
8 x 6 = 48
9 x 6 = 54
10 x 6 = 60
11 x 6 = 66
12 x 6 = 72

List of tables

7x table

1 x 7 = 7
2 x 7 = 14
3 x 7 = 21
4 x 7 = 28
5 x 7 = 35
6 x 7 = 42
7 x 7 = 49
8 x 7 = 56
9 x 7 = 63
10 x 7 = 70
11 x 7 = 77
12 x 7 = 84

8x table

1 x 8 = 8
2 x 8 = 16
3 x 8 = 24
4 x 8 = 32
5 x 8 = 40
6 x 8 = 48
7 x 8 = 56
8 x 8 = 64
9 x 8 = 72
10 x 8 = 80
11 x 8 = 88
12 x 8 = 96

9x table

1 x 9 = 9
2 x 9 = 18
3 x 9 = 27
4 x 9 = 36
5 x 9 = 45
6 x 9 = 54
7 x 9 = 63
8 x 9 = 72
9 x 9 = 81
10 x 9 = 90
11 x 9 = 99
12 x 9 = 108

10x table

1 x 10 = 10
2 x 10 = 20
3 x 10 = 30
4 x 10 = 40
5 x 10 = 50
6 x 10 = 60
7 x 10 = 70
8 x 10 = 80
9 x 10 = 90
10 x 10 = 100
11 x 10 = 110
12 x 10 = 120

11x table

1 x 11 = 11
2 x 11 = 22
3 x 11 = 33
4 x 11 = 44
5 x 11 = 55
6 x 11 = 66
7 x 11 = 77
8 x 11 = 88
9 x 11 = 99
10 x 11 = 110
11 x 11 = 121
12 x 11 = 132

12x table

1 x 12 = 12
2 x 12 = 24
3 x 12 = 36
4 x 12 = 48
5 x 12 = 60
6 x 12 = 72
7 x 12 = 84
8 x 12 = 96
9 x 12 = 108
10 x 12 = 120
11 x 12 = 132
12 x 12 = 144